chapter one

My cousin Nick stomped over to our table. "I don't believe it. My lunch is gone again!" He scowled and sat down. "This is the second time this week."

"You probably just forgot it at home," Robyn suggested.

"No chance. I never forget my lunch," Nick said.

I could relate. By noon I was so hungry, I was ready to eat the linoleum in the school hallway. I never forget my lunch either.

"Hey, Nick! You finished unpacking, yet?" I had to shout to make myself heard over the clanging of metal chairs and the loud voices. Lunch hour in our school was like the monkey house at the zoo. And it didn't smell much better at the moment, either. "Robyn, if you're gonna bring roadkill sandwiches, you have to sit somewhere else."

Robyn flicked her ponytail over her shoulder and took another bite. "It's not roadkill," she answered. "It's liverwurst and onion."

"Augh! Same thing!" I made a face.

Nick grinned hungrily. "At this point, anything looks good." He stared at Robyn's sandwich. Robyn sighed and handed him half.

"Nick, no!" I clutched my hair with both hands. "It's suicide! I'll give you some of mine!"

"I'll take all offers," Nick said with his mouth full. "I'm starving." He took another bite. "And no, we're not finished unpacking. At least Dad found the boxes with my clothes in them last night. Now I can finally change my socks."

Nick had just moved to Calgary a few weeks ago with my aunt and uncle, and was new at my school.

I rummaged in my backpack for my lunch. It seemed kind of empty. I peered inside, then shook it. A bag of carrots fell out. That was all. "Did anyone see my lunch? I brought a ham-and-cheese sub."

Robyn and Nick shook their heads. "Maybe you left it in your locker," Nick said.

"No way. I know I had it," I said. I opened my bag of carrots in disgust and looked at Robyn suspiciously. "If you swiped my lunch because I said your sandwiches smell like roadkill, it's not funny. I could starve to death."

"I never took anything, I swear," Robyn said. She reached into her lunch bag, and a puzzled look crossed her face. "I don't believe it! I brought extra chocolate bars to share with you doofs, but they're missing."

"What!" My stomach rumbled with disappointment. My only lifeline until four o'clock was slipping away. "How can they be gone?"

"You probably ate them already," Nick said.

Robyn shot him a sour look. "I think I'd know if I ate three chocolate bars."

The three of us stared at each other.

"Something very weird is going on," Robyn said.

"Heads up!" someone yelled. Before any of us could move, something hit Robyn in the head. Pink goo splattered everywhere and slimy red things dripped down her hair.

Robyn shrieked. "What *is* this!" she yelled, flicking a red glob onto the table.

I leaned closer and sniffed. "Yogurt," I pronounced. "Strawberry, I think."

"Yogurt!" Robyn turned around and her gaze landed on Cray Simmons, who was at the table directly behind us.

Cray is one of those kids who enjoys stirring up trouble. Me, Robyn and some other kids used to play football with him after lunch, but his mouthy, super-jock attitude really bugged Robyn, so she quit.

He hasn't stopped baiting her since.

Cray's mouth twitched, and I could tell he was trying not to laugh—Robyn was so obviously furious. She *did* look pretty funny.

"Cray! You butt head! I'll get you for that!" Robyn hollered.

"I didn't do it," he said. "Why would I waste my yogurt on you, rich girl?"

"You're such a jerk." Robyn whipped the remains of her sandwich at Cray. His smirk changed to astonishment as bits of liverwurst clung to his shirt.

"Hey!" he said, looking angry. "What the—!"

That's as far as he got.

"Food fight!" someone yelled. Within seconds, the air was thick with flying potato chips, cheezies and other odds and ends. Someone shook a pop and opened it. Wet foam sprayed everywhere. Cray stood paralyzed as bubbling drops trickled down his forehead. A tomato slice hit Nick on the cheek and stuck until he shook it off.

"Ow!" he yelled. He reached for Robyn's

half-empty juice box and prepared to throw it into the fray.

"Stop!" Cray shouted suddenly, recovering movement at last. "Quit being so stupid!" He dove over his table and grabbed Nick's wrist, forcing him to drop the juice box.

Nick shoved him away. "You started it!" He took the remnants of Robyn's sandwich and squished it into Cray's face.

"I did not, butt face!" Cray gasped through the liverwurst. Cray twisted away, a crust of bread dangling from one ear. He tackled Nick. The two of them went down hard and began wrestling under the table. Nick's skinny arms were no match for Cray, and Cray soon grabbed him in a headlock.

"All right! That's enough!" the principal bellowed. Ms. Beaudry marched into the room, and quiet instantly fell, except for the scuffling under our table, where Nick and Cray were still locked in battle.

"Crawley Simmons! Get up, now!" Ms. Beaudry's face was bright red. I could almost see the steam coming from her ears. Cray, who hates being called by his full name, scrambled to his feet. Nick followed, banging his head on the table in the process.

"Fighting again, Cray." Ms. Beaudry frowned. "How many times are we going to go through this? I am *not* impressed. I will see you down in my office. And Nick," she turned to him. "Since this is only your first week here, I'll assume that you will make yourself familiar with our school rules. Fighting will not be tolerated. Is that clear?"

"Yes, ma'am," Nick muttered.

"As for the rest of you...." Ms. Beaudry looked around the room. "This behavior is totally unacceptable. Throwing food is something I would expect of two-year-olds, not junior high students."

"Cray started it," Robyn muttered loud enough for us to hear.

"I did not!" Cray shouted.

"You did so!" Robyn retorted. "He threw an open cup of yogurt at me. Look at my hair!"

Ms. Beaudry regarded Robyn calmly. "Who started this is not the issue. Who participated is the issue. Each one of you will clean up this mess until this place is spotless. If you are late for your first class after lunch, you will make up the time with me at noon tomorrow. I expect every single one of you to serve a week's detention in the library during the lunch hour starting Monday. Is that clear?" She barked the last sentence like an army drill sergeant. The room was silent. "I said, is that clear!"

"Yes," we all muttered.

"Get started." Ms. Beaudry strode out.

Cray followed her without a word. Robyn fumed as she began picking up stray cheezies and stuffing them into her empty lunch bag.

"Hey, wait! Those are still good." Nick stopped her.

"You've got to be kidding! They've been on the floor." Robyn stared at him.

"I'm still hungry." Nick complained.

A look of realization dawned on Robyn's face. "That's it!" she said. "Cray stole your lunches for the food fight! He planned the whole thing!"

"Wait a second, Robyn," I said. "Why would Cray plan a food fight?"

"Because he's a total jerk," she reasoned.

"So?" I shook my head. "And what about your chocolate bars?"

"Well, those are too good to throw around," she reasoned. "He probably kept them."

"Robyn, just because you don't like the guy, you can't accuse him of stealing," I said.

"Well, somebody's stealing," Nick put in. "My stomach will vouch for that."

chapter two

"Robyn, this is dumb," I complained.

"Do you want to keep your lunch or not?" Robyn answered, shoving three large jingle bells inside my lunch bag. She stapled it shut. As I took it, the motion set the bells jangling.

"I feel like Santa Claus," I said.

"Look, if you'd leave your lunch in your locker like everyone else, it wouldn't get stolen so often," Robyn said. My lunch had disappeared four times now.

"If I left my lunch in my locker, I couldn't eat it anyway. Who wants to eat sandwiches that smell like rotten sneakers?" My locker partner must have had the same running shoes since dinosaurs roamed the earth. Anything left in our locker for longer than ten minutes smelled like stinky feet, which was why I carried most of my stuff around with me, including my lunch.

I had to admit that Robyn's idea worked. I still had my lunch at noon, although I'd endured a lot of strange looks and a few ho-ho-ho's.

We still had two days of detention left. Today was Thursday, and Ms. Beaudry had made us march straight to the library at noon to do homework for the last three days—no talking, no goofing around. We were allowed to go to the cafeteria to eat during the last fifteen minutes of lunch, when everyone else was finished.

But today our librarian, Mrs. Pringle, was taking over. She'd said yesterday that she had a special project she needed help with.

Since our school was a new elementary and junior high, we didn't have many books in our collection, and we needed a ton—everything from picturebooks to young adult novels. A bunch of books had been donated to the school, and our job was to help Mrs. Pringle sort through the new material during detention. That was fine with me—anything to get away from Ms. Beaudry's prison-guard stare.

In the library, I put my binder and lunch bag on a table with the other lunches and took a seat beside Nick and Robyn.

"All right, kids," Mrs. Pringle said. "I'm not sure what we have here. A lot of these books are discards from other schools, and some are from schools that have closed. We need to go through them to see what we can use." She opened the cover of a book and showed us where the copyright date was. "Anything older than fifteen years should go in a separate pile, and I'll check it."

"Does that mean if a book is more than fifteen years old, you won't keep it?" I asked.

"No, Trevor," Mrs. Pringle said. "But I need to see what kind of book it is. If it's reference, we might need something more current. There are lots of terrific books that are more than fifteen years old!" She held up an old hardcover copy of *The Lion, the Witch and the Wardrobe* as an example. "For instance, this book was written more than fifty years ago, but it's always been a favorite. I know our elementary students will love it." Mrs. Pringle put the book down on the library cart. "Let's get started."

Nick, Robyn and I started working through the nearest box. Most of the books were out-of-date textbooks or encyclopedias from the eighties.

"Why weren't these books given away ages ago?" Robyn wanted to know, brushing dust off her hands.

"Who knows?" I said. "Probably no one got around to it."

"This box is hopeless," Robyn said. "There's nothing in here we can use." She flipped the pages of an ancient math text in disgust.

I reached into the box and pulled out a huge science book, noticing a second book wedged inside the tattered book jacket. "Hey, what's this?" I said. I pried the jacket loose and released a thin, hardcover book with a color picture of a hockey player on the cover. The book dropped onto my desk, falling open to a well-thumbed photo of a player wearing a blue and orange uniform. My jaw dropped.

"What is it?" Robyn wanted to know.

I hesitated. "It's a hockey book from 1980."

"Oh." Nick looked bored. He's not big on sports. "That's pretty old. Mrs. Pringle will probably want to chuck it out." He slid his chair back and went to grab his lunch.

"I don't think so," I said slowly. I recognized the player and the uniform right away. So did Cray. He stopped stacking books on the table and peered over my shoulder.

"That's Wayne Gretzky when he first played with the Oilers," Cray said with interest.

"So what? Who asked you to butt in?" Robyn said.

"It's a free country, princess," Cray informed her.

Robyn gritted her teeth. "And you're free to leave. Take a hike, Cray."

Cray deliberately leaned against my desk and folded his arms across his chest, ignoring Robyn. "Gretzky is one of the best hockey players that ever skated in the NHL." Cray said. "He won the Hart Memorial Trophy for MVP in his first season in the NHL."

"Which makes this even more cool." I pointed to the signature on the page.

"He signed it? That's awesome," said Cray. "That book must be worth thousands."

"How would you know?" Robyn said rudely.

"I've collected sports stuff for years," Cray told me, still ignoring Robyn. "I've bought some hockey stuff on Internet auctions before, and anything to do with Gretzky is worth big money, especially if it's rare."

Mrs. Pringle came to investigate. "Look what we found," I said. I lifted the photo so she could see. "Cray thinks it's worth some serious cash."

Mrs. Pringle picked the book up as though she were handling diamonds. "It might be," she said. She checked the copyright date, then the photo. "This was signed after his first season with the Oilers. See the caption under the photo?" She showed us. "That's more than twenty-five years ago."

"Wow." Cray shook his head. "This is unbelievable."

"It's a real piece of hockey history, all right," Mrs. Pringle said.

"Do you think our school will be able to keep it?" Robyn asked.

"No, I'm sure it will go on display somewhere. But maybe we'll be allowed to keep it for a little while." Mrs. Pringle smoothed the cover with her hand and glanced at the clock. "You kids are done. Go have your lunch."

I got up in relief. My stomach was so empty, I thought it was going to cave in. A sudden cry erupted from the table where the lunches were piled. Nick's face was red and his hands were empty. "Someone," he yelled, "has ripped off my banana and marshmallow-fluff sandwich!"

Robyn sighed. "Not again!"

Cray was busy looking through a nearby stack of books. Robyn eyed him suspiciously as we walked out of the library. She took half of her pickle sandwich from her lunch bag and handed it to Nick in the hall. "I wonder," she said, "why my lunch doesn't get stolen."

"Because you bring such weird stuff," Nick said, his mouth full. "Not that I'm not grateful," he added, as Robyn glared at him. "But not many people like pickle sandwiches."

chapter three

"There really isn't any choice. You'll have to get rid of most of them," Mrs. Pringle said.

Nick stopped to tie his shoelaces in the library doorway, dropping his overdue books on the ground. Robyn stopped so suddenly behind him that I collided with her, sending her stumbling into Nick.

"Trevor!" she said in a furious whisper.

"I couldn't help it. What's the matter, anyway?" I said. Mr. Kowalski and the rest of our grade eight class should have been right behind us, but the hall was still empty.

"Shhh. I want to hear." Robyn cocked her head toward the library interior.

Mrs. Pringle sighed. "I know. It was nice to get the donation, but most of these books are terribly out-of-date. We need new materials so badly. Building up a library takes time, but these kids need books *now*."

I peered around the doorway and saw her talking to Ms. Thorsen, the new grade nine teacher. Unlike Mrs. Pringle, who was plump and wore her graying hair clipped back, Ms. Thorsen looked trendy with square black-rimmed glasses and short blond hair. I could almost imagine her as a DJ at a rock station.

Ms. Thorsen glanced into one of the boxes of books that was stacked on the floor. "There's no budget left?"

"Not much. A big chunk of it went to buying computer equipment. We'll need more money if we want books this year."

Robyn burst into the library. "Mrs. Pringle, I know! We could have a fundraiser to buy books!"

Mrs. Pringle and Ms. Thorsen turned in surprise. Robyn's face turned pink. "We were just coming in and heard what you said," she explained as Nick and I followed her in.

Robyn continued. "We could raise the money," she said. "It wouldn't be hard. The school always has fundraisers."

"Well, it's a great idea, Robyn, but that's just the problem. We do have a lot of fundraisers, and our parent council does most of them. I'm not sure we could get the support for another one."

"Why couldn't we do it ourselves?" Robyn persisted. "Trevor, Nick and I could do most of the organizing if you're too busy."

"We could?" Nick looked startled.

Robyn elbowed him hard in the ribs. "Yes, we could. I bet we could get other students to help. It would be fun."

"Yeah, loads," Nick muttered, just loud enough for me to hear.

Mrs. Pringle hesitated. "I don't know, Robyn. It would be a lot of work to get it organized for this school year, and I'm not sure I'll be here next year. It might be better to wait until September."

"But we need books now. You said so," Robyn pointed out. "What if we held a literacy fair? The whole school could help!" Her eyes lit up. "We could have a used book sale. We could sell all the donated books that the library can't use!"

"That's a great idea, Robyn!" Ms. Thorsen said enthusiastically.

"It would solve the problem of getting rid of these discards." Mrs. Pringle glanced at the boxes full of books. "But there's still a lot of books no one will buy—old textbooks and things."

"That's easy. We can donate those to charity." Robyn gave an airy wave of her hand, then stopped. "But wait a minute, Mrs. Pringle. What do you mean, you won't be here next year?"

Mrs. Pringle frowned. "I shouldn't have said that. It slipped out before I thought. I don't really know for sure. But with more students coming in for fall, there may not be room in the budget for a librarian."

"That's terrible!" Robyn cried.

Mrs. Pringle smiled, but her eyes looked worried. "That's the way it is, honey. There's only so much money, and teachers are necessities. The school can manage without a librarian."

"I can't!" Robyn burst out. Anger made her swell up like a toad. "Librarians are important!"

Mr. Kowalski, his curly brown hair more disheveled than usual, strode through the library door with the students. "Sorry, kids," he said to us. "I had a phone call. The rest of the class had to wait. Have they been any trouble?" he asked Mrs. Pringle.

"Not at all." She smiled. "Quite the opposite. While we were waiting, Robyn, Nick and Trevor volunteered to spearhead a literacy fair to raise money for the library."

Mr. Kowalski took a sip from his coffee cup and wiped his bushy mustache. "Really? That's sounds great. Let's see if they can put the same resourcefulness toward their social studies project." He faced the class. "Find a computer, kids, and get started. We only have twenty minutes left before lunch."

I sat down at the nearest computer station and logged on. I only had time to type in my outline before Mr. Kowalski interrupted us.

"Everybody, stop and save, please. We have to pack up. It's almost time for lunch." He glanced at the clock. "Sorry this session was so short. I'll see if I can book some extra time on the computers this afternoon with Mrs. Pringle."

The bell sounded. Nick slammed his binder shut. "Let's go! I'm starving."

Robyn caught up to us in the hall, just as we passed the school office. Her gaze fastened on a grade seven boy who was standing near the office door. He was shifting uneasily from foot to foot and hiding something behind his back.

"Look!" Robyn whispered. She gestured toward the boy.

I looked. "So?"

"So, he's up to something!" she hissed. "Can't you see what he's hiding?"

I stared. It was a lunch box—a pink lunch box with sparkly stars. The boy caught me looking, and his face turned red.

"He could be the lunch thief," Robyn insisted. "Look at how he's acting. He's very nervous. That's suspicious, if you ask me."

"Yeah, but..." I started to object, but Robyn took off like a shot.

She strode up to the boy and demanded, "Where did you get that?"

The boy gulped. "Get what?"

"That lunch box."

"What lunch box?"

"The one behind your back!"

The hall was crowded with students, and people turned to see what was going on. "I...um—" The boy started to sweat. He looked around wildly, as if searching for escape.

Robyn glared at him. "You stole it, didn't you? You're the thief who's been ripping off lunches, aren't you?"

His face went blank. "I have no clue what you're talking about, but I didn't steal anything, so mind your own business!"

At that moment, a small, curly-haired girl wearing a pink denim jumper came up.

"Thanks, Connor," she said, taking the lunch box from him.

"The next time you forget your lunch, get Mom to bring it. Okay, Holly?" The boy said through clenched teeth.

"Okay," the girl chirped. She skipped back to her class.

Connor gave Robyn a baleful glance and took off down the hall. Robyn turned back to us, completely crestfallen.

"Don't worry, Robyn," I said, fighting back laughter. "Even the best detectives make mistakes." Nick kept his face turned carefully away and was making weird snuffling noises in an effort to control his own urge to laugh.

"Stop it, you morons," Robyn scowled at us.

"You're calling *us* morons?" Nick sputtered, finally giving in to a fit of laughter. It was contagious, and I couldn't hold it in any longer. Loud guffaws erupted from both of us. The madder Robyn looked, the funnier it seemed. Nick doubled over and had to lean one arm on the wall for support.

She glared at us, her hands on her hips. "So tell me, brainiacs. Why was he hiding the lunch box, if it belonged to his sister?"

Nick snorted. "Think about it, Robyn. No guy wants to stand in the hall holding a pink lunch box. That's like holding a sign that says, 'I'm a dweeb.'"

"Oh." Robyn paused. "I never thought of that."

I managed to stop laughing. "You're a girl. Pink lunch boxes aren't a big deal to you."

"Okay, so I was wrong." Robyn shrugged. "I still think it's Cray, anyway, but a good detective has to investigate every possibility," she said in a pompous voice. "Come on, let's go eat."

chapter four

"What's the next move, Sherlock?" I asked Robyn.

"Stick it up your nose, Trev," she answered. We were back in the library working on our research project. "The guy with the pink lunch box looked suspicious, so I investigated. Which is better than *you*—sitting on your butt doing nothing. It's your lunch issue that I'm trying to solve, you know."

"I'm not doing nothing," I retorted.

"Yeah, you are," Robyn said. "I'm doing all the work, and no one's swiping *my* lunch."

"That's because it's disgusting," Nick interrupted. "And the next move is for someone to explain to me why I can't get this dumb Internet to work."

"Need some help?" A grade nine boy from Ms. Thorsen's class stopped, his arms full of books. Their class was organizing the new books for Mrs. Pringle.

"Sure." Nick gestured to the screen. "I can't get the search engine to work."

"No problem." The boy set down the books. Some old detective novels were on top of the pile. I have a weakness for high-action mystery-thrillers, even fifty-year-old ultra-cheesy ones. This one was titled, *Mac Dougall and the Case of the Monster From Mars.* I opened the cover, but the boy looked up. "Hey, don't mess with those."

Surprised, I stopped. "I was just looking at it."

"Sorry, but I just finished sorting them. I don't want them to get mixed up."

I raised one eyebrow and caught Robyn's eye. She shrugged.

He turned back to Nick.

"Anyway, I think you're putting in the wrong keywords. Try something like this." The boy typed rapidly for a moment.

"Blake, what are you doing?" Ms. Thorsen asked.

"Just helping this guy for a second on the Internet."

Mrs. Pringle came over to see. "What's the problem?"

"Nothing," Blake answered. "I fixed it." He explained to Nick what he'd done.

"This is majorly cool," Nick enthused. He scrolled through several pages. "Look at how much stuff came up."

Mrs. Pringle shook her head. "I can't keep up with all the technology."

"That's what happens when you were born in the Dark Ages," Blake said, grinning. "Right, Mom?"

Mrs. Pringle gave him a teasing frown. "Get back to class." She moved away to finish packing a box of discards. Blake scooped up his books and went over to help Ms. Thorsen.

"That's Mrs. Pringle's son," Robyn hissed.

"Brilliant deduction, Holmes," Nick said, typing intently.

Robyn shot him a withering stare. "I just never knew that."

"Me neither," I said. "I wonder...," I paused as Ms. Thorsen stopped at our table.

"Less talking, more working. Trevor, I think you need to be at a different computer station. Come with me."

Reluctantly, I stood up and followed Ms. Thorsen. She wove around a table stacked with books in the far corner and turned on the computer stationed behind it.

"There you go," she said.

Annoyed, I plunked myself into the chair and waited to log on. I was surrounded by a fortress of books that cut me off from Nick and Robyn. Some of the books were part of the series of Mac Dougall detective novels that Blake had been sorting. They were really ancient—the kind without a book jacket, just an illustrated hardcover.

I picked one up and flipped through the yellowed pages. A slip of paper fell out. It was a note covered with pencil-jotted numbers, but before I had a chance to look at them too closely, Mrs. Pringle appeared over one of the book towers.

"Trevor," she said, "could you help me lift this box onto the trolley? It's too heavy for one person."

"Sure." I shoved the note into my jean pocket and heaved one end of the box. It was filled to the brim with books. We staggered under the weight and placed it carefully on the trolley.

"Thanks," Mrs. Pringle said, brushing the dust from her hands. "I think I over-packed that one."

She noticed the detective novel I'd been looking at and smiled. "I used to like that series. Mac Dougall and his friends always got themselves into terrible trouble. I'd have to read under the covers with a flashlight, because I couldn't wait to find out how they got out of it. It's a shame I have to discard them."

"Why do you have to?" I asked.

"Well, the books are getting too old to be lent out—they'd start falling apart. I don't think many kids would be interested in them, anyway."

"Do you..." I hesitated. "Do you think I could have one, then? If you're getting rid of them?"

Mrs. Pringle paused, then grinned. "Sure. But don't tell anyone, okay? If Robyn gets her way, these books will go into the used book sale. If everyone decides they want one, we won't have anything left to sell!"

"Okay." I tucked the book—*Mac Dougall and the Secret of the Underwater Spy*—inside my binder.

"Now, you'd better get to work before class is over." Mrs. Pringle took two stacks of books and walked away to pack them, leaving a hole in my wall of books. I could see Nick still typing at his computer, his eyes glued to the screen. Robyn was flipping the pages of a magazine.

I sighed and entered my password. Research projects were not my favorite thing to do. Searching the Internet is fun, but writing up the report afterward is harder. I plugged a few keywords into the search engine and waited while the computer looked them up.

Ms. Thorsen was rummaging through stuff on the trolley, where Mrs. Pringle and I had loaded the heavy box of books. When I heard her gasp, I peeked around a book stack to see what the problem was.

She had her square glasses propped up on top of her head, and she was chewing on her bottom lip. "What's the matter?" Mrs. Pringle asked, coming over.

"The hockey book—the one with Gretzky's signature—it was here on the cart."

"I know. I was going to put it in my office after I showed it to your class," Mrs. Pringle said.

"It's gone!" Ms. Thorsen whispered.

"Gone!" Mrs. Pringle stared at her, wide-eyed. "What do you mean?"

"I mean, it's not here. Look."

Mrs. Pringle rifled through the books on the cart. "Oh, no!" She looked at Ms. Thorsen in dismay. "What are we going to do?"

Ms. Thorsen rubbed her forehead. "We start looking," she said grimly.

chapter five

"Hey!" Ms. Thorsen yelped. I dodged her at the last second.

The heavy box she was carrying teetered in her arms. I grabbed for it, but I must have done the wrong thing because the cardboard bottom collapsed and a cascade of books spilled onto the floor.

"No running in the halls, Trevor," Ms. Thorsen said crossly, picking up scattered books.

"Sorry, Ms. Thorsen," I said. I reassembled

the box and began stuffing books inside. I caught a glimpse of a hockey picture before Ms. Thorsen scooped up several books and pulled the box farther away from me.

She straightened her Oilers ball cap. She was dressed in running tights and a T-shirt, to exercise during the lunch hour.

"Oilers fan?" I said.

Ms. Thorsen grinned at the disapproval in my voice. "Is that a problem?"

"The Flames are way better," I said.

Ms. Thorsen didn't argue. She just picked up the box. "Thanks for helping clean up." The noon bell rang, and she headed for the door to the parking lot.

A stream of kids poured into the hall. I went to my locker to grab my lunch, trying to ignore the smell of putrid sneakers that burst out as I opened the door. Rachel Gibbons shared this locker with me, and her feet were brutal. Everything in this locker came out smelling horrible.

Our locker would not normally win awards for neatness, but today it might have qualified as the world's messiest. I rummaged through the piles of crumpled worksheets, textbooks, gym clothes, gloves, and mountains of Rachel's stuff, but my lunch was nowhere to be found. Meanwhile, I nearly passed out from the fumes.

"Trevor! You are such a *slob*." Rachel stomped up behind me. "Look at this mess! I came early this morning and cleaned this locker, and now look at it. It's disgusting! And it stinks too. The Board of Health is going to close the school because your gym clothes are contaminating the air."

"Oh, yeah? I don't think so. You should check your feet," I retorted. "Your sneakers smell like toxic waste!"

Rachel put her hands on her hips, but before she could say anything else, I butted in. "Did you just say you cleaned the locker this morning?"

"Yes." She eyed me coldly. "It took me twenty minutes before the bell just to shovel out all your junk," she said.

"But, Rach," I shook my head, "it was like this when I opened it."

"Give me a break."

"No, I'm serious."

"Well, it was organized when I left it," Rachel answered.

"That means," I said slowly, "that someone's been in here. Did you lock it?"

Rachel looked a little shamefaced. "Well, I never do, actually. I just close the lock. I don't click it shut."

"What!" I felt my eyes bug out. "Why not?"

"Because I can never get the lock open when I'm in a hurry. It always jams," Rachel said defensively.

"Rachel, are you brain-dead?" I demanded. "That explains why my lunch is always missing, even when I leave it in my locker. And that explains this mess. But what I don't get is why? What were they looking for?"

"I don't know, but this means our locker has to be cleaned out all over again, and *I'm* not doing it this time." Rachel elbowed past me, grabbed her lunch out of her backpack inside the locker and flounced off.

"What's going on?" Nick tapped my shoulder. Robyn was just behind him.

"Someone trashed my locker," I said. "Rachel said she just cleaned it this morning, so someone's definitely been into it."

Nick peered into the mess. "Anything missing?"

"Besides my lunch, I don't know yet."

"My lunch is gone too. Someone swiped my pickle sandwich," Robyn fumed. "I just know it's Cray. We'd better catch that bozo before the entire school starves. I bet he took that hockey book too. Mrs. Pringle told me it's still missing."

"Come on, Robyn," I said. "Just because you don't like the guy doesn't mean he's a thief."

"Look at the facts, Trevor," Robyn retorted. "He starts a food fight after he stockpiles lunches, he's totally into hockey, and when Mrs. Pringle showed us that book about Gretzky, he thought it was majorly cool. What more do you want?"

"Evidence, maybe?" Nick said.

"I don't understand why you guys don't believe me." Robyn frowned. "He thinks it's fun to pick on other kids. He's probably laughing every time one of us is stuck at lunch with nothing to eat."

"I don't know, Robyn," I said. "He's not really that bad."

"Hah." Robyn snorted. "That's what you think."

"Robyn, you have to come up with facts, not opinions," said Nick.

"Okay. It's a fact that Cray Simmons is a jerk. What more do you want?" Robyn answered.

Nick groaned.

"Shh." I nudged Robyn. I'd spotted Cray coming down the hall.

"Hey, Trev," he said. He noticed Nick and Robyn watching him. "What are you staring at?"

"We're just wondering whose lunch you'll rip off next," Robyn said.

"I don't know what you're talking about, Princess." But Cray's ears turned deep red.

"Oh, yeah. I think you do," said Robyn. "And I'm sick of losing my lunch."

"If throwing up is a problem," Cray snickered, "maybe you shouldn't bring those gross pickle sandwiches."

"Ah-hah!" Robyn yelled, pointing her finger at him in triumph. "You *are* the thief. How else would you know I bring pickle sandwiches?"

Cray hesitated, and then he put on a sneer. "Everyone knows you bring gross sandwiches. It's a fact."

"He's right, Robyn," I said, ignoring her glare.

"Okay, well what about the missing library book? What did you do with the Gretzky book, Cray? Sell it on the black market?" Robyn demanded.

"What's your problem, anyway?" Cray's face turned a mottled purple, and his mouth was an angry line. "I didn't take any library book! So just shut up!" Cray pushed past us and stomped away.

"You see?" Robyn turned to us. "Guilty. He wouldn't be so mad if he wasn't."

"Oh, for Pete's sake, Robyn!" I threw my hands up in the air. "That doesn't mean anything. You'd be mad too, if someone accused you of something."

"Not if I hadn't done it."

"Especially if you hadn't done it," Nick pointed out. "People don't like being called liars."

Robyn looked stubborn. "I still think it's Cray who's behind all this."

"I keep telling you, you need proof," I said. "Without proof, you've got nothing."

"There could be a lot of people in this school who would steal lunches," Nick added. "Maybe it's one of the teachers. Maybe it's me...lunches didn't start disappearing until I showed up at this school."

"That is so dumb," Robyn said. "You were the first one to have your lunch stolen. Why would you starve to death, if you were swiping lunches?" Robyn shook her head. "I'm telling you, it's Cray. And if you guys don't think so, then prove it."

"How are we supposed to do that?" I asked.

"You read all the detective novels," Robyn challenged. "Think of something!"

"Yeah, Trev." Nick grinned at me. "Think of something."

chapter six

"Hey, Robyn!" I called to her from the school office door, where she was doing lunch duty. Some students help out in the office over lunch, while the staff eats. Today it was Robyn's turn.

"Just a second. I have to get this call." She answered the office phone. "Brookside School. Can I help you?" She scribbled something on a notepad. "Thank you for getting back to us. All right. I'll let her know." Robyn hung up, her face beaming. "Plans for the literacy fair are really taking off, Trev. That was one of the parents Mrs. Pringle contacted. They know a professional storyteller who might be able to come."

"That's great," I said with as much enthusiasm as I could muster.

The secretary walked by, her keys still in her hand. She smiled. "Thanks, Robyn. I can take over now." Robyn slid out from the chair behind the desk, just as a grade one girl pushed through the doorway.

"I don't feel good," the girl announced. And then, with a retch that came from her toenails, she threw up all over the office floor.

"Oh!" Robyn jumped back to avoid getting splashed.

The secretary dropped her keys and coat on the nearest chair and took the little girl by the shoulder. "It's okay, honey. Let's take you into the nurse's office, and you can lie down til your mom or dad gets here."

"Okay," sobbed the girl, before she threw up again. The office phone buzzed insistently. The secretary looked harassed.

"Robyn, could you answer that, please?" She grabbed an empty wastebasket and held it in front of the girl as she led the way to the nurse's room.

I lifted the front of my T-shirt up over my nose. "I'll wait for you outside."

"Thanks a lot!" Robyn said, annoyed. She picked her way around the puddle on the floor and reached for the phone. I stood in the hall where the fumes weren't so bad, and after a couple of minutes, Robyn hurried out.

"That was a really weird phone call," she said.

"What do you mean?"

"Well, the guy said he was just talking to someone who called from here. He got cut off, so he dialed the number on his call display and got the main office. He said if I could find out who had called him, to let the person know that his business doesn't handle items like that for resale, but an auction house might. Or Internet sales."

"What items?"

"He didn't tell me."

"And he didn't say who the message was for?"

"He didn't get a name. So I wrote down the message, but I have no clue who it's for. It was just weird."

"Never mind. The teachers will figure it out. Come on, we're late."

Mr. Kowalski was letting Nick, Robyn and me skip science to have a literacy fair planning session in the library. Mrs. Pringle was supposed to help us get started.

Nick was already there, working at a computer station. I sat down next to him. Robyn flipped open her binder and ripped out a fresh sheet of paper.

"Okay," she said. "Besides the used book sale, what ideas do we have so far? Do you think a poet's corner would work? Or should we focus on fiction?"

"Sure," I said, bored.

"Which one? Sure isn't an answer that applies to my question, Trevor," Robyn said.

"Whatever."

Robyn threw her eraser at me. "I mean it, doofus. This is serious."

"Did you guys know how many search engines are on the Net?" Nick interrupted. "I have about a million hits for the keyword hockey."

"Why are you looking up hockey?" I asked. "You hate hockey."

Mrs. Pringle pushed the library cart past us. "I'll be with you kids in a minute," she said and began shelving books in the picturebook section.

"What if she gets fired?" Robyn said, abruptly changing the subject.

"Who?" I glanced up, startled.

Robyn nodded toward the librarian. "Mrs. Pringle."

I put my pen down. "What are you talking about?" I said in exasperation.

"Open your eyes, Trev," Robyn answered. "She's really upset about losing that book. She was responsible for it. Gretzky's signature on that old hockey book makes it really rare. Maybe it's worth so much money that she might lose her job."

"I doubt it," I said, but I felt a twinge of uncertainty. Mrs. Pringle was already worried about whether she would still have her job next year. What if this was reason enough to fire her? "That can't happen. We need her."

Robyn shrugged. "I know. But that means someone's got to find that book."

Nick and I shared a look.

"Haven't we got enough to do, trying to find the lunch thief and organizing the literacy fair?" Nick asked.

"Do you want Mrs. Pringle gone forever, her reputation tarnished? She'd never get another job if she's charged with theft. She'll end up with no money, no house, stuffing old newspapers into her boots to keep her feet warm in the winter!" Robyn's voice rose. She sniffed.

I rolled my eyes. "Robyn, get a grip! No one's talking about a crime, here."

"How do you know? Maybe someone took that book and tried to sell it," Robyn retorted.

"And how would a person sell something like that, Robyn? A garage sale?" I shook my head.

Nick broke in. "Actually, Trev, Robyn's on to something. People sell stuff over the

Internet all the time. There are cyber stores and auctions just for selling used junk. I'll bet you could sell antiques or a collector's item for a lot of money online."

Robyn stared. "That guy who called the office mentioned Internet sales."

"That could be anything, Robyn. A teacher selling a car maybe. It doesn't mean someone is trying to unload the Gretzky book for big money."

Robyn was unconvinced. "It's too much of a coincidence, Trev," she argued.

"Mrs. Pringle's son showed me how you do all these advanced searches. Let's find out," Nick broke in. He began punching the computer keyboard. The machine whirred softly for a few seconds. He frowned. "Nothing there. Let's try hockey collectibles."

It took Nick five or six tries with different keywords before a cyber bookstore came up with a match.

"Look." He swiveled the screen so we could see. The bookstore had a listing for the same hockey book we had.

"Out of print. What does that mean?" Robyn wanted to know.

"They don't publish it anymore," I said. "That's why it's worth more."

"No kidding," Nick said, scrolling down the screen. His eyes bugged out at the total. "This book is worth almost four hundred dollars!"

"No," I said slowly. "I don't think so."

"Yeah. Look!" He pointed to the screen.

"It's worth more," I said. "Ours is signed, so that makes it even more valuable. I'll bet that stolen hockey book is worth at least twice as much that—probably about eight hundred bucks!"

chapter seven

After school, I held my knapsack upside down and shook it. A few forgotten school notices fluttered out, but that was all. I dropped it on the hallway floor and began pulling stuff out of my locker, piling it around my feet.

"What is going on?" Robyn and Nick walked up behind me.

I couldn't speak—I was holding my breath against the fumes. I held Rachel's sneakers by the shoelaces and dropped them a safe distance away.

"Fumigating," I said at last. I began searching the locker again. "I can't find the book Mrs. Pringle gave me."

"What book?" asked Nick.

"An old detective novel that she was going to discard. She had a whole series of them, and she said I could keep one."

"Maybe you took it home," Robyn suggested.

"No, I'm sure I didn't. I already checked."

"Left it in class?" she asked.

"Nope. It was here, Robyn. I remember leaving it in here."

"Maybe Rachel has it."

"I doubt it," I said. "She isn't exactly into that type of reading. Someone's taken it."

"Why?" Robyn asked.

I shrugged. "Who knows? But Rachel leaves the lock undone on our locker a lot. Anyone could have gotten into it."

"Like Cray," Robyn said.

I shook my head. "Robyn, lay off the guy, will you? We have no proof."

"No, but we're about to," said Nick. "I have a plan."

"But I had a plan," Robyn said.

"Well, I said I had a plan first, so get in line," Nick said.

"Hmmph," Robyn grumped. "It had better be good."

"It is," Nick said. "And, it's foolproof."

"Nick, look out!" Robyn yelled. We were in my kitchen, putting Nick's idea into place. Robyn jumped back as Nick squeezed the container. Blue food dye splattered down the front of her jeans and left bright blue splotches on the kitchen linoleum.

"Oh, that's just great." She surveyed her jeans. "It looks like I've been attacked by a blueberry bush, and this stuff doesn't wash out."

"Well, if you'd held the eyedropper steady, I wouldn't have spilled it. Besides, I did you a favor. The blue dye covers up all those bleach marks on your pants."

"They're supposed to be there, you doofus!" Robyn yelled.

"My mom will kill me if she sees this floor," I said, grabbing some cleanser from under the sink. I began to scrub the stains on the linoleum. The blue marks disappeared, and I breathed a sigh of relief.

Nick picked up the eyedropper. "I'll hold it this time. You pour," he said to Robyn.

Robyn tipped the plastic bottle, letting the food dye drip slowly into the eyedropper. When it was full, she capped the bottle and picked up the package of Twinkies on the counter. "Now what?" she asked.

"Now," Nick said, "we rig the Twinkie." He slit the edge of the package, slid out one of the small cakes and hollowed out some of the cream filling with a toothpick. Then he inserted the eyedropper and gently squeezed the blue food coloring into the middle. Nick dabbed a bit of the extra cream filling to cover the hole, then replaced the Twinkie in the package and glued it shut. "There!" he said. "The lunch bag bandit will never be able to resist this—and then, we have him, red-handed."

I grinned. "You mean, blue-lipped."

"You hope," Robyn said doubtfully.

"Okay, this is it," Nick whispered. The booby-trapped Twinkie had disappeared, along with the rest of my lunch, right on schedule. Nick was pumped that his plan might actually work.

I was almost able to ignore my hunger pangs and choke down part of Robyn's pickle sandwich. It might not have been so bad, if she hadn't run out of cheese and used ketchup instead.

"This is totally gross, Robyn," I said, gagging.

"Think of it as a hamburger, without the meat." Robyn took a bite.

"Somehow, that doesn't help," I said. I surveyed the green and red filling inside the bun, and put it down in disgust. I looked around the lunchroom. In a lot of schools, different age groups eat at separate times, but our school has enough room to let everyone eat together. So far, I hadn't seen any Twinkies, but junk food is inhaled so fast around here, it's hard to tell who's eating what.

"You know," Robyn said. "There's no guarantee that Cray—I mean, whoever took Trevor's lunch—is going to eat it at school. They could eat it outside, or toss it in the garbage or something."

Nick looked worried. "I hadn't thought of that."

"Or what if the blue dye doesn't squirt out of the Twinkie? We'll have to check inside everyone's mouth," Robyn continued. "We'll be like the mouth police. Open up! Lemme see your teeth!"

Nick frowned at her, but at that moment, a commotion erupted at one of the elementary tables. We all rushed over, but Robyn got there first.

A freckle-faced grade four boy sat there, his face frozen with shock. His lips and chin were stained blue, and the tampered Twinkie lay half eaten on the table, oozing blue filling.

Robyn glared at Cray, who was watching the scene from close by. I could see she was stunned that he wasn't the culprit, but she pulled herself together.

"Where did you get that Twinkie?" she asked the boy.

"I don't know!" the boy wailed.

"What do you mean, you don't know?" Robyn demanded. "It doesn't belong to you, does it?"

"Someone gave it to me!" The boy tried to wipe the blue off his face, but only smeared it more. His chin wobbled, and I could tell he was trying hard not to cry. Everyone in the lunchroom was staring at us now.

"Oh, get real!" Robyn said.

"Take it easy, Robyn," I murmured.

Cray could keep quiet no longer. "Back off, rich girl. You're bothering the kid."

"Quit calling me that!" Robyn snapped. "I'm *not* rich. And this kid is in possession of a stolen Twinkie."

Cray snorted at that, which only made Robyn madder.

"Who asked you to butt in, anyway?" she yelled.

"I don't sit back and do nothing while someone bullies younger kids, Robyn," Cray shot back.

"I'm not bullying him. He's been stealing lunches, and I want to know why," Robyn said fiercely.

"No, I haven't!" the boy wailed.

"Quit picking on him!" Cray clenched his fists. "He didn't take anything!"

Robyn turned. "How would you know?"

"Because, rich girl." Cray met her stare. "*I* did it."

chapter eight

"So you *are* the lunch bandit! I knew it!" Robyn said. She'd been right, and I knew we'd never hear the last of it.

"Yeah, so what?" Cray answered belligerently.

"So, you owe us about fifty lunches, that's what!" Robyn yelled.

"What's going on?" Ms. Thorsen, who was doing lunchroom supervision, strode over. Then she saw the tearful grade four boy with bright blue lips. "What happened to you? Is that ink? Did you swallow any of that?" she asked, beginning to panic. The boy nodded.

"Oh, no!" She began to propel the boy toward the door.

"Wait! Wait, Ms. Thorsen!" Robyn hollered. "It's okay. It's only food coloring!"

Ms. Thorsen stopped dead in her tracks. "What?"

"It's food coloring."

"Why does he have food coloring all over his face?" Ms. Thorsen asked ominously.

"He ate a booby-trapped Twinkie," Nick explained.

Ms. Thorsen blinked. "What—?" She stopped, studied Cray's angry face and Robyn's triumphant expression, then glanced at the now-silent lunchroom. All the kids had stopped eating and were waiting to see what would happen.

"I want all of you..." she eyed me, Robyn, Nick, Cray and the boy with blue lips, "...to explain this in my classroom. *Now*."

We followed her out the lunchroom door.

I carried the stolen Twinkie.

Once we were inside Ms. Thorsen's classroom, she pointed to the desks. "Sit," she said angrily.

We sat.

"Who's responsible for this?" demanded Ms. Thorsen, pointing at the Twinkie, which was now oozing bright blue icing. It looked pretty disgusting, actually.

"We are," Robyn said. "Trevor, Nick and I."

Ms. Thorsen fixed us with a stare that could sear flesh from bone. "Playing practical jokes that humiliate younger students will not be tolerated," Ms. Thorsen's voice was tight with outrage. "I am very disappointed in you kids."

"It wasn't a practical joke!" protested Robyn.

"Then explain," Ms. Thorsen snapped.

Robyn and Cray spoke at once, but between them all that came out was gibberish.

Ms. Thorsen held up her hand. "You first." She pointed at Robyn.

"Someone's been stealing our lunches. Trevor even had his locker broken into. So, we decided to catch whoever was taking our food. We put blue food coloring inside a Twinkie so that when the thief bit into it, we'd have proof."

"I see," said Ms. Thorsen. "So why are you saying Cray is the thief?"

"Because he gave the Twinkie to this boy," Robyn said. "Cray admitted it."

"Is that true?" Ms. Thorsen asked Cray.

"Yeah," Cray said, glaring at Robyn.

"Why?"

"Because."

Ms. Thorsen crossed her arms. "You must have a reason, Cray, and no one leaves this room until we hear it."

Cray just shrugged, but he looked at the floor and refused to meet Ms. Thorsen's eyes.

"There's no way you've been pigging out on five or six sandwiches every day," Robyn said.

"He's not," the grade four boy said. He'd been so silent, I'd almost forgotten he was there. "He's been giving food to me and my sister and some other kids."

"Why?" Robyn asked.

The boy turned away and didn't answer.

"Because they don't get much for lunch, that's why," Cray answered.

Everyone was silent, even Robyn.

"I remember what that's like. Last year, both my mom and dad were out of work for a couple of months. We didn't have much extra money, so my lunch was thin, man. I was lucky if I had a sandwich. No juice, no fruit, and for sure no Twinkies."

"So you decided to steal food from other people?" Robyn said in disbelief. "How do you figure making us go hungry is any better?"

"Because you're not really hungry. Face it, Robyn. None of you is going to starve. I see kids dumping stuff from their lunch in the trash all the time. So what's the difference if I take it and give it to someone who really needs it?"

"Stealing is wrong," Robyn said, but her voice lacked conviction.

"Starving is wrong too," Cray shot back.

"Cray..." Ms. Thorsen hesitated. "Why didn't you tell someone? The teachers could have helped. There are emergency lunches in the office for students who've forgotten theirs."

"Yeah, but that's not for every day," Cray said. "And it's not like I can bring enough food from home. I had to swipe lunches."

Ms. Thorsen looked thoughtful. "Cray, I understand why you did this, but you still took things from other people. You opened lockers that didn't belong to you—"

"I only did that twice," Cray interrupted. "And that's because Trevor's locker partner leaves the lock open." He looked at me. "Your locker is brutal, man."

I grinned. "Why do you think I hardly ever leave my lunch in it?"

"Every other time, I took stuff that was just lying around," Cray said.

Robyn couldn't contain herself. "Lunches that are left on a table while we're working in the library aren't exactly lying around, Cray."

Cray shrugged. "Whatever."

"And what about the Gretzky book?" Robyn demanded. "What did you do with that?"

"I never took that!" Cray said fiercely. "Look, I know the Gretzky book is worth a wad, but I still never touched it. So you can just shut up, princess!"

Ms. Thorsen held up her hand.

"Stop it," she said. "Let me finish. Cray, there are other ways to solve this problem. I think we need to talk to the principal and see what can be done."

"So that's it?" Robyn said. "He's not even going to get in trouble?"

"No, that's not all," Ms. Thorsen said firmly. "All of you will serve another week's detention at lunch hour—Cray, for stealing lunches, even if it was for a good cause, and you three for rigging the Twinkie. Vigilantism is *not* encouraged at this school, and tampering with food can be dangerous. I'll also be speaking with your parents. You kids can go now, but don't let me catch you doing something like this again!"

Robyn made a sour face as we walked toward the door. "I'll bring extra for your friends," she muttered into Cray's ear before we left. "But if I ever catch you swiping my pickle sandwiches again, Cray, you are roadkill."

"Don't worry, Robyn," Cray whispered back. "That's exactly what your sandwiches taste like!"

chapter nine

The man wore a dark suit, shiny black shoes and a drab tie.

"Who is that guy?" Robyn whispered, staring as he walked past. Lunch hour was almost over and we were in the library, serving yet another day of detention. We'd been working on posters for the literacy fair.

"I have no idea. He doesn't look like a teacher," I answered.

"He's going over to the desk," Robyn said in a low voice.

"Let's get closer." I dropped down and crawled on all fours behind the shelves, past the entire nonfiction section. Robyn followed me. I squirmed up against the picturebook display next to Mrs. Pringle's desk area. I stared at the cover of a Curious George book and listened.

"Arlene Pringle?" the man said. I peered out and saw him shake Mrs. Pringle's hand. "I'm Ron Shaw. I'm here to appraise the artifact you found."

"The artifact?" Mrs. Pringle's eyes widened.

"Yes. I understand you found a vintage hockey book with Gretzky's signature. Your principal asked me to authenticate the signature."

"Oh...uh, yes. We did." Mrs. Pringle's face flushed. "It's...quite unfortunately...not at the school today. I'm afraid I didn't know you were coming."

Robyn sucked in her breath and dug her elbow into my ribs.

The man frowned. "Is there any way to get the artifact here?"

"No, I'm afraid not," Mrs. Pringle said.

"I don't like to waste my time," he grouched.

"Then next time I suggest you make an appointment," Mrs. Pringle said crisply.

"Good for you, Mrs. Pringle!" Robyn whispered.

The man turned on his heel and walked out.

Mrs. Pringle's face appeared over the picturebook display. "You two can come out now."

Robyn stood up and brushed off her knees. "How did you know we were back here?"

"Teachers know everything." Mrs. Pringle smiled.

"We have to find that hockey book," I said.

"I know." Mrs. Pringle looked worried. "It was my responsibility, and I think it's quite valuable. I hope it turns up soon."

"So do we," Robyn assured her. "We'll find it, don't worry."

"You kids go eat lunch, before noon hour is over," Mrs. Pringle said.

We found Nick in the lunchroom, fresh from detention in Ms. Thorsen's room, where he'd been stapling science worksheets into booklets.

"It was awful. The desk was piled three feet high with paper," he moaned, relishing his salami, mustard-and-hot-sauce-submarine sandwich. He'd already given half the sub, plus a juice box, to our grade four Twinkie victim. Robyn had donated oatmeal cookies, and I gave him an apple before school started this morning. That kid had been eating like a king since the Twinkie episode, but we all felt good about it. Stealing is one thing but sharing is another.

We told Nick what had happened in the library. "The missing lunches were no big deal compared to Mrs. Pringle losing her job," Robyn concluded. "The Gretzky book is valuable, and Mrs. Pringle is going to take the blame for losing it. We have to get it back."

"I don't see how. It could be anywhere," Nick said with his mouth full.

"We look for clues, Nick," Robyn said.

"There aren't any," Nick said.

"Yes, there are. There always are," Robyn insisted.

I dumped the contents of my lunch bag on the table. "Okay, let's look at what we have. Cray turns out to be the lunch thief, but swears he had nothing to do with the hockey book. We have no other suspects, no other evidence, and no way to trap the culprit, since the book disappeared over a week ago."

I shook my head, but then I remembered when I bumped into Ms. Thorsen in the hall and she dropped her box of books. I'd seen a hockey book in that scattered pile, before she scooped everything up. She was pretty mad, and she wouldn't let me help, either. "Wait a minute," I said. "Maybe we do have another suspect." I briefly told Robyn and Nick what had happened.

"Ms. Thorsen?" Robyn said in disbelief. "You've got to be kidding."

"Well, think about it. I know what I saw, Robyn." I remembered something else. "And you know what?" I said. "She was wearing an Oilers cap that day."

"So what?" Robyn said.

I rolled my eyes. "Robyn! The Oilers! Hockey! The team Wayne Gretzky played for when he signed that book."

"Oh."

"We need to find a way to check out those books," I said. Blake Pringle threw some stuff in the trashcan nearby, and he paused when he heard what I was saying. "Hey, Blake, you're in Ms. Thorsen's class, right?"

"Yeah. So?" Blake answered.

"So, we need to find out where she took a box of books from the library last week," I said.

"She has three boxes full of them in the classroom."

"Really?" I wondered. I'd seen her going toward the doors to the parking lot that day. I thought those books would be long gone.

"Yeah, we helped her take them out to her car last week, but nothing fit. Her car is stuffed with junk. She said she'd have to wait until she cleaned out her car to take them to the Salvation Army."

"That's great!" I said with enthusiasm. Blake gave me a weird look. "I mean, we just need to look through them."

Blake shook his head. "She's pretty testy about those books. She keeps yelling at us to quit messing with them. I don't know if she'd let you look at them."

I exchanged glances with Robyn. "It's really important," Robyn said. "We think the missing hockey book with Gretzky's signature might be in one of the boxes."

Blake looked thoughtful. "And you don't want to ask, because you don't want Ms. Thorsen to find out you think she's the thief." Blake gave us a sly grin. "Sounds like fun. I think I can find a way to help you guys out."

"Ow! Trevor, get your elbow out of my ear!" Robyn whispered, giving me a jab with her finger that nearly separated my ribs.

I tried to move away from Robyn, who was crouched on the floor. "Nick, you're standing on my toe," I said.

"Sorry. I can't see a thing." Nick shuffled to the side.

"Shhhh!" Blake whispered. "I think she's leaving."

The four of us were stuffed into a broom closet just outside Ms. Thorsen's classroom after school. She'd helped a student with a homework problem and talked to a parent about someone's grades. Now we were waiting for her to leave for home.

Ms. Thorsen's heels clicked down the hall. As the sound faded, we unraveled ourselves and burst out of the broom closet like microwave popcorn from the bag.

"She's gone. Come on," Blake whispered. "They're back here."

The boxes were stacked neatly with the cardboard tops folded shut. We wrenched them open and began taking the books out. Within about thirty seconds, all three boxes were dumped on the floor.

"We'll never get this put back the way she had it," Robyn looked at the sea of books in despair.

"Never mind. Just start looking." I sifted

through the books. There were textbooks, old paperbacks and hardcover book jackets in all colors with pictures of everything under the sun, *except* hockey.

"Any luck?" Nick called out. He was stationed at the classroom door, keeping a lookout.

"Not yet," I said.

"Start tossing the books you've checked back into the boxes," Robyn suggested. "That way we can narrow the search."

Blake showed only mild interest, leafing through the books nearest him. Robyn and I worked at a frenzied pace, spurred on by the knowledge that Ms. Thorsen was likely to fry our butts if we were caught after the Twinkie episode.

"Are you sure you saw the Gretzky book in here, Trev?" Robyn asked.

"I saw a hockey picture. That's all I know." I stacked a set of almanacs from the 1970s, and then threw some old romance novels on top.

We tossed several armloads of books into the boxes, but the Gretzky book was nowhere to be found. I looked at Robyn dismally. She shrugged, and then froze as Nick gestured frantically.

"You guys!" he hissed. "Hide!"

Too late. The door opened.

"What is going on here?" I felt my blood turn to ice. Ms. Thorsen was back.

We were caught.

chapter ten

Shock rooted us to the spot. Ms. Thorsen regarded us calmly, but I read the anger in her eyes. "What are you kids doing?"

We had no choice but to explain. We didn't accuse Ms. Thorsen of actually stealing the Gretzky book. We just said that we were worried it had been packed by mistake.

"Do you honestly think I wouldn't double-check these boxes myself?" Ms. Thorsen said crossly. "And really, how many detentions do I have to give you before you get it through your heads that this detective work is a bad idea?"

Only if you don't suspect a teacher, I thought but didn't say.

"All of you just earned another week of lunch-hour detention. I know you're trying to find the missing Gretzky book, and I appreciate the effort, but it's not here! If I catch you guys messing around where you shouldn't be again, we will be discussing suspension with the principal. Now clean this mess up and go home for supper." Ms. Thorsen's eyeballs bulged. "And Blake, don't even tell me why you're here. Explain it to your mother. She's waiting for you in the library. Go. *Now*."

Ms. Thorsen narrowed her gaze as Nick, Robyn, and I cleared up the rest of the scattered books. "You know, if you guys worked as hard at schoolwork as you do at solving mysteries, you'd be on the honor roll," she said as we left her classroom.

"Yeah," Robyn muttered. "Except that we can't seem to solve anything. Nice going, Trevor."

"What do you mean?" I demanded.

"You said that you saw the Gretzky book when Ms. Thorsen dropped the box in the hallway."

"No, I said I saw a hockey picture. I never said I was sure. Besides, this was a dumb idea. If Ms. Thorsen did take the Gretzky book, do you really think she'd keep it with the other books? Not likely. She probably took it home, or hid it in the classroom."

"We can't risk staking out her classroom again," Nick said. "If we're caught, we'll get suspended for sure."

"But we don't have any real clues," Robyn complained. She zipped up her jacket as we walked outside.

"I wish we'd had more time." A raw wind blew icy snow into our faces. I jammed my hands into my jeans pockets. "We might have found something if Ms. Thorsen hadn't come back." I felt a papery lump in my pocket and pulled it out, hoping it was money. Instead it was a folded note that had obviously been through the laundry.

"What's that?" Robyn asked.

"I don't know." I unfolded it carefully. A row of numbers was still legible on the paper, in spite of the washing machine. "It's not homework, and it's not my handwriting."

Robyn leaned over my shoulder. "Those are ISBN numbers. I remember them from when we sorted books for Mrs. Pringle. Where did you get this?"

I thought for a minute before I remembered. "It was in the detective novel that Mrs. Pringle gave me. It fell out, and I stuffed it in my pocket."

"The detective novel that's missing?" Robyn said. Her eyes widened.

"Yeah."

"Don't you think that's kind of a coincidence?" she asked.

"What are ISBN numbers?" Nick wanted to know.

"They're like serial numbers. They're a way of keeping track of books," Robyn said. "Look, there's a dollar amount beside each number." They ranged in price from fifty to four hundred dollars.

"So, if we looked up these numbers on the website of an Internet store, the books would come up?" Nick said slowly.

"Probably." Robyn and Nick stared at each other.

"What are you guys talking about?" I said.

"It's a clue!" Robyn shouted. "I know it! Come on, let's go. My house is closest. We can look it up there." She took off running through the icy snow. Nick sprinted after her, and I was close behind.

Robyn burst through her front door, kicked off her shoes and raced into the family room, where the computer sat on a desk in the corner. Nick and I followed her. Robyn's dad poked his head out of the kitchen, where he was cooking supper—spaghetti, judging from the great smell in the house. My stomach growled just thinking about it.

"Robyn?" he called.

"Hi, Dad!" she answered. "Nick and Trevor are here. We need to look up something on the computer for school."

"Okay."

Nick booted up the computer and clicked the mouse on the Internet icon. Then he searched for a cyber-bookstore. "Give me that note, Trevor. I'll type in the numbers."

We could only search one number at a time, but each one was a book from the detective series that Mrs. Pringle was tossing out. Every book was out of print, and some were more expensive than others. Nick tallied up the prices and wrote down the titles. When he had plugged in the final ISBN number, he started adding up the total amount. Nick frowned and erased, then frowned again.

"I don't believe it," Nick said at last.

"What?" Robyn and I said together.

"Those books—if you have the whole series—are worth over five thousand dollars!"

"*What!*" Robyn cried.

"No wonder someone took that book out of my locker," I said.

Nick's voice was serious. "Someone in our school knows about this. The Gretzky book is valuable too, but it's nothing compared with this."

A sharp realization stabbed through me. "Yeah, and who in our school knows a lot about books?" I said.

"I don't know. Who?" Nick asked.

I paused. "Mrs. Pringle!"

"No way, Trevor." Robyn shook her head. "There's no way."

"Think about it, Robyn. No one but us knows those discards are worth a ton. But she would! She knows all about books, and she'd never get caught, because everyone else thinks they're worthless. It makes total sense!" I said.

"Yeah, except she gave you one of those books," Robyn pointed out.

"Maybe she didn't know how much they were worth then," I said.

"She must have," Nick argued. "There are prices on that list."

"Well, why would she risk her job by taking the Gretzky book?" Robyn persisted.

"That I don't know," I answered. "Unless she thought the risk was worth it. Maybe she figured she was going to lose her job anyway, so why not take the money and run?"

"I don't believe it," Robyn said stubbornly. "Mrs. Pringle is too nice. She'd never do anything like that."

"Robyn, whether you like someone or not doesn't change the facts. You thought Cray was behind everything, just because you don't like the guy. Well, he did swipe lunches, but not for the reasons you thought, and he never touched those books."

"That hasn't been proven, yet," Robyn interrupted.

"And now," I continued. "You don't believe Mrs. Pringle could do anything wrong, just because you think she's great!"

"Look, you guys," Nick broke in. "Let's just say Mrs. Pringle does have the books. Where would she hide them?"

"Not in the library, because they could get mixed up with the other books," I said.

"I don't think she would leave them in the school," Nick mulled. "It would be too risky, with the literacy fair and everything. Someone could pack them up for the sale."

"You guys are nuts," Robyn said.

"I'll tell you where I'd hide them. In my car!" I said.

"Mrs. Pringle drives a van. There'd be plenty of room," Nick added.

Something tugged at my memory. "And I'll bet they're still there. Mrs. Pringle had to get me to help her load boxes of the discards onto a trolley. There's no way she could get those boxes out of her van without help."

Nick and I looked at each other.

"No way! No way are we breaking into her van." Robyn shook her head.

"She's working late tonight organizing all the donated books," I said.

"Are you out of your mind?" Robyn demanded. "We just got nailed for staking out Ms. Thorsen's classroom, and you want to add car prowling to the list?"

"We don't have a choice!" I argued. "Are you going to let her get away with five grand?"

"You don't know it's really Mrs. Pringle!" Robyn said hotly.

"We don't have any suspects left, Robyn," Nick replied. "If you have another one, let's hear it."

Robyn remained glumly silent, but Nick and I nodded at each other.

"Let's go!" We jumped to our feet.

chapter eleven

We ran through the icy darkness toward the school, our sneakers pounding on the sidewalk. It was only 5:30, but the early winter sun had already set. The street lamps made pools of light on the road.

"Do you think she'll still be there?" Robyn puffed.

"Probably," I wheezed. "Mrs. Pringle was still working when we left, and that was less than an hour ago."

There were a few lights on in the school, but the parking lot was dark and nearly empty. Mrs. Pringle's van was in the farthest corner.

"That's great," Nick whispered. "No one can see us trying to get inside."

"That's because no one can see, period," Robyn complained. "Did anyone bring a flashlight?"

"Uh...no," Nick and I answered.

Robyn sighed. "Well, this is useless. The windows are tinted and we can't see a thing. So now what?"

"Check the doors?" Nick suggested.

"You can't do that!" Robyn said. "That's trespassing."

"What do you think we're here for?" Nick said in disbelief. "A tea party?"

"If Mrs. Pringle really has the stolen books, she could get in a lot of trouble," I said.

"So could we!" Robyn retorted as Nick tried the door handle.

The door swung open with a rusty creak. I swallowed. "See anything?" I said as Nick climbed inside.

"Not yet."

I peered into the interior. Nick had moved to the back and was searching the trunk area by feeling along the walls and floor. I craned my neck to see if there was anything in the passenger seat and then stepped inside to help Nick.

"Nothing," Nick said.

I was about to check under the seats, when I heard the crunch of gravel.

"Someone's coming!" Robyn hissed.

I leaped backward in panic, bashing my head on the doorframe. Nick tripped over me and we fell out the door, landing on Robyn. The three of us collapsed in a heap.

"Get off!" Robyn shoved me. She leaped to her feet and closed the door as gently as possible. Nick yanked me to my feet.

"Run!" he said.

My head throbbing, we ran as hard as we could, until we disappeared into the blackness at the edge of the parking lot.

"You know, you guys," Robyn said the next morning as we walked down the school hallway toward the library, "since we caught Cray stealing lunches, we haven't found proof of anything, except that someone stole Trevor's detective novel and the whole set is worth a ton of money. The Gretzky book has been missing for ages. All we've done is nearly get suspended. So much for your brilliant plans."

"Well, Ms. Sherlock," Nick said, "have you got any better ideas?"

"Actually, yes," Robyn answered smugly. She pushed open the library door. "I do."

Nick and I looked at her. "And?" I said. "What is it?"

But Robyn gasped. Her eyes widened and the color drained from her face. "Look!" she croaked. She took off running through the library at top speed.

I stared at Nick. He shrugged. "We followed Robyn. She had collared a younger kid—he couldn't have been older than seven— and had pulled a book from his arms.

"Hey!" the boy cried. "That's mine!"

"No, it isn't," Robyn said. "Where did you get this?" She held it up so Nick and I could see. It was the missing Gretzky book.

"From here," the boy said in disgust, as if the question was so obvious anyone should know the answer. "I took it out."

"You stole it, you mean?" Robyn said.

"No. I borrowed it," the boy answered. "That's what you do in a library."

"Did you sign it out?" Robyn's eyes narrowed.

"Sure. I used my library card."

"But you couldn't have. It doesn't have any bar codes or anything." Robyn flipped open the cover.

"I signed my name on the card in the back," the boy said stubbornly.

A look of understanding crossed Robyn's face. "You signed the old card, from the library that had this book a long time ago!"

"So?" the boy said.

"We need to talk to Mrs. Pringle." Robyn's voice was decisive. She marched over to the librarian's desk, just as Mrs. Pringle came in.

"What's going on?" Mrs. Pringle asked, setting down a stack of papers.

Robyn held up the book and explained. Relief and joy flooded Mrs. Pringle's face. She took the book and held it tightly. "I'm so glad you found it!" she exclaimed.

By now, the younger boy understood. "I'm sorry I took it," he said. "I just really like hockey. I didn't know it was old."

"That's all right," Mrs. Pringle patted his shoulder. "It was a mistake, that's all. I'll help you find another book about hockey that I bet you'll like even better. Okay?"

The boy's face brightened. "Okay."

"Thank you, Robyn, for finding it," Mrs. Pringle said. She led the younger boy away to the nonfiction section.

"I guess that wraps up that mystery," Nick said in relief. "Which is good, because I need to work on my research project. It's due tomorrow, and I need to use the Internet."

"You need to use the Internet, all right, but not for your project," Robyn said. "Have you forgotten about Trevor's missing detective novel?"

"Oh, come on, Robyn," Nick complained. "Three mysteries are too much for any detective to solve. Trevor probably flushed the book down the toilet or something."

"He did not! Someone broke into his locker and took it, and we know the series is worth about five thousand dollars. That money should belong to the school. We could use it to pay part of Mrs. Pringle's salary if the school has to cut her job."

"I don't think they would let us do that," I said.

"Well, we could buy new books for the library, at least. Tons of them, for five thousand bucks," Robyn said.

Nick sighed. "Okay, Robyn. What do you want us to do?"

"First, we need to find out if the detective series is missing from the books that were dropped off at the Salvation Army," Robyn said. "I brought change to call from the pay phones by the office."

"We have class," Nick said.

"We can't wait. Tell Mr. Kowalski we need to be excused for a few minutes for the literacy fair. Make something up."

Nick shot her an exasperated look, but

he left. Robyn led the way down the hall, reached the lobby pay phone, and began leafing through the phone book attached to the base. She deposited the coins and began dialing.

"Hello. I'm wondering if you could check some items that were dropped off from our school." Robyn listened, and then told the clerk the name of the school. "You have? That's great! We think some books we need were donated by mistake."

Robyn turned to me. "What's the name of the series?" I told her, and she gave the information to the clerk.

"Okay," she said after a few moments. "Yes, thank you very much." She hung up the phone, her eyes bright with excitement. "They have the books from the school, and the detective series isn't there. The lady checked twice for me."

"So that means...," I said.

"Someone else has them," Nick finished, catching up in time to hear Robyn's comment.

"Mrs. Pringle has probably taken them

somewhere to sell. They weren't in the van," I said.

"Not if she's using the Internet," Nick answered. "Think about it. Books like that don't get sold in a second-hand store. They're probably antiques, and the best way to find someone who's interested in buying them would be on the Net."

"It's not Mrs. Pringle," Robyn argued. "I still think Ms. Thorsen's been acting weird." We walked back down the hall toward the library.

"It could be Ms. Thorsen," I agreed, "but really, it could be anyone. The principal, for instance."

"That's dumb," Robyn said. "Why would Ms. Beaudry take the books?"

"I'm not saying she did. I'm just saying that we have no proof, and the best way to find those books is to search the Internet auctions and see if someone's put them up for sale. Nick, do you know how to do that?" I pushed open the library door.

Nick shook his head. "I know how to do searches, and probably find those auctions, but I have no idea how to find buyers and sellers."

I thought for a minute, then spotted someone logging onto one of the library computers. "I know someone who does."

"Oh yeah?" Robyn said skeptically. "Who?"

chapter twelve

"Cray." I motioned toward the computer station, where Cray had sat down. "Cray knows how Internet auctions work. He said so, that day I found the Gretzky book. He said he'd bought hockey stuff over the Internet."

"No way!" Robyn exploded. "Not Cray! He's a suspect!"

"Not anymore. Come on, Robyn. So the guy ripped off some food—he was giving it to kids who don't have much for lunch."

"I still don't trust him."

"We don't have much choice. We can't exactly go to a teacher and tell them that we suspect two of their friends of rare book fraud," Nick said.

I walked over to where Cray was working. "Hi," I said.

"Hey." Cray didn't look up.

"Nick and Robyn and I need your help."

"Yeah? That's a switch," Cray said.

"I know...but it's really important." I explained about someone stealing the detective series from the school.

"If Mrs. Pringle was going to give the books away anyhow, who cares?"

"That money should belong to the school. It could help buy books, or maybe start a lunch program for the kids you were trying to help," I said.

Cray finally glanced at me. "Really?"

"Well, maybe. But first we need to find the books."

"Okay." Cray sighed. "What do you need me to do?"

"Search the Internet auctions, see if you

can find out if they're up for sale." I told him the name of the series.

"No problem." Cray punched a few buttons on the keyboard. I pulled up a seat and watched. Robyn and Nick had drifted over and now were looking over my shoulder.

"This one's not bringing much up," Cray said. "There's some of the books you want, but I'll try a Canadian site. We might have more luck there." He tapped away for a few seconds, and then waited as the computer whirred.

"Bingo!" Cray pointed at the screen. "The full series." His eyes widened. "They want fifty-five hundred dollars for it?"

"Yeah. That'd buy a lot of Twinkies," I said.

Cray grinned. "You got it." He double-clicked on the listing. "This sale is from here in Calgary, and the auction closes in two hours, eleven minutes. This is probably your guy," Cray said.

"Or girl," I added.

"What do we do?" Nick asked Cray.

"So now Cray makes all the decisions?" Robyn spat. "This is so stupid."

"You asked for my help, princess. I can log off any time." Cray leaned back in his chair.

Robyn glowered at him.

"Place a bid," I said. "And tell whoever it is we want to meet today to close the deal. Can you do that, Cray?"

"Sure. I'll just send an e-mail with the bid. What do you want to offer?"

"Six thousand dollars. That way no one can scoop us," I said.

"But a bid is a legal thing, man. Where are you going to come up with six grand if this guy's for real?" asked Cray.

"Say we need to meet and check out the condition of the books before we buy, but that we would offer six thousand dollars," I said, "Then we're not stuck with it."

"Okay. Where do you want to meet?" asked Cray.

"The mall, after school today," I said. "It's public and busy, and we can get out of there if we need to."

"Done." Cray clicked the mouse.

"Shhh. Get down!" Robyn put the flat of her hand on top of Nick's head and pushed him behind a potted palm. "We don't want anyone to recognize us."

"No one will recognize you, that's for sure," I said. Robyn wore a toque pulled down over her ears, her winter coat with the collar turned up, and sunglasses. "Aren't you hot?" The mall must have been at least a hundred degrees. People were wearing T-shirts inside. We were stationed behind a pillar with several plants, watching the food court. Cray said in the e-mail that we would meet the seller in front of the pizza place.

"What if they didn't get the message?" Robyn worried.

"They will," Cray said. "If the auction closed today, they'll be checking the bids."

"Well then, what if someone bids more than—" Robyn stopped as I nudged her with my elbow. Someone wearing a winter jacket and toque was carrying a large box toward the pizza place.

"This is it!" Nick whispered.

"Let's go." I bolted out from behind the pillar. When I was behind the person, I cleared my throat. "Hey!"

The figure turned, and I recognized who it was immediately. It wasn't Mrs. Pringle. It wasn't even Ms. Thorsen.

"Blake!" Robyn gasped. "What are you doing here?"

Blake Pringle nearly dropped his box of books. "Wh-what's up, guys?"

"Nothing. Just a little detective work, if you know what we mean," Nick said, plucking one of the novels out of the box.

Blake paled. "I don't know what you're talking about."

"Oh, yeah? Six thousand dollars is a lot of money, Blake. What were you going to do with it?" I asked.

Blake contemplated me for a second, then shoved the box at me and ran. I juggled the box, tripping over Nick's feet. Nick lost his balance and ended up sprawled on the floor. Robyn took off running, but her heavy coat and flopping toque were affecting her speed. Cray took a flying leap, flung both arms around Blake's ankles, and brought him down.

"Thanks, Cray," Robyn gasped as the three of us caught up.

"No problem." Cray got up, brushing off his palms. Blake still lay in a painful heap, but he got up slowly, wincing.

"Don't run," Cray warned.

"You can't prove anything," Blake said defiantly. "I'll erase all the files from the auction. No one will ever know, and it'll be my word against yours."

A mall security officer brushed through the small crowd of spectators that we had attracted. "Okay, kids. We don't allow fighting in the mall. I'm going to have to contact your parents. Come with me please."

"Oh, no." Cray cursed.

But a second figure pushed through the crowd. "What's going on, here?"

"Ms. Thorsen!" Robyn cried.

That teacher was like gum on our shoes. We just couldn't shake her. But this time, I was really glad to see her.

"How did you know we were here?" Robyn asked.

Ms. Thorsen frowned. "I was already at the mall when I saw you kids, and I recognized the box of books. I thought I'd better see what was going on." She turned to the security officer. "These are my students. I can take them home."

The officer wavered, but then a call came over his walkie-talkie about a group of shoplifters in the drugstore. "Okay. But make sure their parents are aware of the situation."

"I will," Ms. Thorsen said grimly. She towed Blake and Cray off to the side of the mall. Robyn, Nick and I followed. "Explain."

Robyn filled her in.

"Your mom's not going to be very happy with you." Ms. Thorsen looked at Blake.

"Yeah, well...I did it to help her," Blake muttered.

Ms. Thorsen looked startled. "Help her with what?"

"She might lose her job next year, and I

know she's worried." Blake frowned. "I just thought...well, six thousand dollars would help a lot."

"But you were stealing!" Robyn said.

"I was not!" Blake flared. "The school was going to get rid of the books, anyway. So who cares if I took them?"

"That money should belong to the school, and you know it," Robyn retorted. "Mrs. Pringle would never take that money."

"How do you know? She isn't your mom!" Blake fired back.

Ms. Thorsen regarded Blake for a long moment. "Come on," she said. "Let's get you kids home."

chapter thirteen

"Nick, pass me the tape, would you?" Robyn called from the table where she was working. A whole bunch of kids, including Nick, Robyn, Cray and I, were helping with the week-long literacy fair. Since we still didn't know if Mrs. Pringle would be at our school next year, Ms. Thorsen decided to get things rolling. We were going to have storytelling, a used book sale and a carnival of reading games.

We had parent volunteers, whole classrooms digging up used books, posters, and an advertisement in the school newsletter. Mrs. Pringle had been right, it was a lot of work.

Robyn brushed her hands off on her jeans, leaving a trail of silver sparkles from the poster she'd just finished. "What do you think?" she said, showing me the poster. It was a picture of a kid reading a book, with a castle and dragon in a thought bubble.

"It's great," I said. "But you got the date wrong."

"What!" Robyn panicked and checked the poster. "I did not, you doofus!"

"I think it's wonderful," Mrs. Pringle said, coming up behind us. "And I wanted to thank you kids for caring enough about me to try to find that hockey book. The school has decided to keep the Gretzky book, and it will go in a glass display in our library."

"What about—" Robyn started, and then stopped herself.

"The detective series?" Mrs. Pringle finished. "Well, I've talked to the principal.

We've decided to sell the series and put the money toward a lunch program for kids who need it."

"Really?" Cray perked up. "That's great!"

Mrs. Pringle smiled. "And whatever the literacy fair raises will go to new books for our library, so everything's turned out just fine."

Robyn frowned. "Except that we still don't know if you'll be at our school next year."

"It doesn't seem as important now, after what Blake did," Mrs. Pringle said. "He worried so much about it—and look what happened."

"Is he in a lot of trouble?" Robyn ventured.

"Enough," Mrs. Pringle said grimly. "But the school isn't pressing charges. The truth is, I really would have tossed those books out, thinking they were worthless. So it's funny, if Blake hadn't taken them, the school wouldn't be getting any money."

We were silent for a second, thinking about that.

"I'm hungry," Nick said at last.

Robyn reached into her backpack. "I have half a pickle sandwich left from lunch." She unwrapped the wax paper and held it out.

Nick looked at it with distaste. "Yuck, Robyn. You forgot the cheese again."

Robyn took a bite with relish, but Cray grabbed his own backpack. "That reminds me. I brought a snack just for you guys," he said.

Nick sighed with relief. Cray pulled a box out of his backpack and ripped it open. He grinned and held up a plastic-wrapped package.

"Blue Twinkies, anyone?"

Like her character, Trevor, **Michele Martin Bossley** loved reading mystery novels as a child. She still has her collection of books in the Trixie Beldon series. This award-winning author has written more than a dozen children's sports books, including *Jumper* in the Orca Sports series. Michele lives in Calgary, Alberta.